# THE FACE OF JESUS

R. NELSON PRIKRYL

**Quantum Discovery**
A LITERARY AGENCY

ISBN
978-1-958690-79-6 (Paperback)
978-1-958690-80-2 (eBook)
978-1-958690-78-9 (Hardcover)

"...seek His face continually."
1 Chronicles 16:11

# TABLE OF CONTENTS

Acknowledgments ........................................................... vi

Introduction................................................................ vii

Chapter 1   The Face............................................................. 1

Chapter 2   The Temple in Nature................................... 13

Chapter 3   The Ark............................................................ 21

Chapter 4   Tithe ............................................................... 27

     Part 1 ...................................................................... 28

     Part 2 ...................................................................... 33

Chapter 5   Geography....................................................... 37

Chapter 6   Mazzaroth[5]...................................................... 41

Chapter 7   Revival ............................................................ 49

Chapter 8   The Signs ........................................................ 59

     Part 1 ...................................................................... 60

     Part 2 ...................................................................... 65

     Part 3 ...................................................................... 67

Chapter 9   In the Numbers............................................... 69

Chapter 10  Life.................................................................. 77

     Part 1 ...................................................................... 78

     Part 2 ...................................................................... 82

Epilogue...................................................................... 85

Conclusion.................................................................. 89

Bibliography................................................................ 90

About the Author....................................................... 91

# ACKNOWLEDGMENTS

I want to thank my wonderful wife, Sue, and my good friend, Perry T. Stakes III. It was their never-ending interest and encouragement that brought these ideas to print.

# INTRODUCTION

This book was birthed out of a burden for people. A burden for their souls and for answers to their problems. I'm not interested in debating theological issues that, one, you may never learn the answer to; and two, or even if you do, it will not help anyone. One does not need a lot of theology to get to heaven, but it helps in this world to learn all available wisdom. Perhaps you will find the design of everything interesting. Maybe you will think that God has a sense of humor. I hope that I've dealt with this subject with all due respect for we are stepping onto holy ground.

There are ideas in this book that I've looked at in a different manner. I did so because it seems to reveal an order to things. Things are interconnected. This is unfortunately not seen in matters of faith, but it is true. Everything is interrelated.

When God's Word symbolizes two or more things by the same symbol, they are related. There are many examples, and I have yet to find an exception. The is also true of things God created that look alike.

It is a great joy to share with you some ideas from the Bible. This book was written at a level that everyone can enjoy.

If you are wondering what you can gain from this book, I have a few suggestions. If you are a Christian, don't miss chapter 1. I hope it will help you understand your salvation. If you are an agnostic, don't miss chapters 2 and 6. You will find interesting patterns in the design of nature. If you are a Jew, don't miss chapters 3, 6, and 8. If you are in business, chapter 9 addresses maximum sales and profits. If you are a nuclear chemist or physicist, find His face in the nucleus in chapter 2. If you are a student, His face is in circles, ellipses, parabola, and hyperbolas in chapter 9.

Regardless of who you are, I hope this book will help you begin or deepen your life with the Lord. No matter what your philosophy, there is one point where everything important comes together and resolves itself. I believe that His face cannot be overestimated. It is absolutely universal. It is there that we can find life.

If you wish to read from your personal Bible, scripture references are set in bold type. I hope you receive as much joy as I did in the discovery of these ideas.

## CHAPTER 1

# THE FACE

This discussion is more of an explanation than proof though it has elements of both. I believe that His face is so profound that it unites and explains everything. It does not matter whether you are Jewish, Muslim, agnostic, or atheist or whether you are into science, art, business, farming, or home care. It does not matter from which culture you came. Whatever your background is, His face can resolve your questions. Whether those are philosophical questions, practical questions, theological questions, or personal questions, your answer is in His face.

This book was not intended to be a book on apologetics, but there is apologetics present. It was not intended to be a book on evangelism, but evangelism is present. It is a book that shows that everything is interwoven; nothing is an accident, and in His face is the answer to everything. It is by understanding of His face that we can understand everything else.

In chapter 1, the reader is invited to travel with me through a variety of biblical events that give illustration to the connection between His face and wisdom, marriage, marital relations, and birth. We will well see that there is something very special about it.

\* \* \* \* \*

The face of Jesus has three properties:

1. It unites everything in Scripture and nature.
2. It explains everything.
3. It is the key to the parallel of marriage and Christ and the church.

The last property is the key to the first two. We will discuss what His face is literally like but not what He looks like. Then we can understand it symbolically.

**For this cause shall a man leave his father and mother, and shall be joined unto his wife, and they two shall be one flesh.**

**This is a great mystery; but I speak concerning Christ and the church.** (Ephesians 5:31-32)

Everything that exists, from economics to astronomy to nuclear physics and geography, is a parable built on this theme. Marriage is a picture of Christ and the church. The key to this picture is the face of Jesus. His face is the dynamic that bonds Christ and the church in one spirit. This spiritual bond is similar to the physical bond that creates one flesh. It is mysterious. It is a hidden thing.

**In the light of the king's countenance is life.**[1] (Proverbs 16:15)

Life is a key to the unity of everything in Scripture. Where is life? In the face of the king. Who is the king? Jesus. Thus, life is in the face of Jesus. Now, what exactly is life?

**And this is life eternal, that they might know [ginosko] thee, the only true God and Jesus Christ whom thou has sent.** (John 17:3)

Life is to know God and Jesus Christ, and life is in the face of the King. Observe what Mary said when the angel Gabriel told her she was to have a son named Jesus: **"How shall this be since I know [ginosko] not a man?"** (Luke 1:34). *Ginosko* is obviously referring to a marital union. Luke used the same Greek word *ginosko* that John used in John 17:3. Thus, there is a parallel of one spirit producing eternal life and one flesh producing physical life.

In Luke 1:35, the angel said, **"The power of the Highest shall over shadow thee,"** and Mary said, **"Be it unto me according to thy word"**

---

[1] The Hebrew word for countenance literally means face.

3

(Luke 1:38). When Jesus called the Word the good seed, the Greek word used is *sperma*. The Word of God is like the seed of man. Thus, the Word of God is the agency of spiritual reproduction.

We will see that the Word will be compared to other things, but this comparison seems to take priority. It is the background for the others.

So far, we have shown His face as an intimate bond between Christ and the church as a picture of marriage.

We can find that the Bible also makes an analogy of marital love and the Spirit. It does this by comparing both of them to wine. To see the face of Jesus is to be bonded to Him in a oneness of spirit that parallels one flesh in marriage.

**Let him kiss me with the kisses of his mouth; for thy love is better than wine.** (Song of Solomon 1:2)

In many places, including Acts 2 and Ephesians 5:18, the Spirit is compared to wine.

**And be not drunk with wine...but be filled with the Spirit.** (Ephesians 5:18)

This means that there is an analogy of marital love and the Spirit. Thus, it seems that the Spirit is one reason that His face parallels marital love.

This seems to be the reason for the events in John 2. After receiving the Spirit, His first miracle was turning water into wine at a wedding in Cana.

When the believers see the face of Jesus, the relationship will be consummated. Having established the vital nature of His face, we can turn to many other things and see the idea of marriage and children. There are four main parts:

1. Monthly cycle/ovulation
2. Gestation
3. Travail and birth
4. Postpartum

First, we have two small things to consider. The last thing Jesus did with His disciples was the Passover. When they drank the cup, they became set apart for Him. In the same way, a Jewish man proposes love. If she drinks the cup, she is set apart (sanctified) for him.

Marriage is depicted again in Acts 11:26: **"The disciples were called Christian first in Antioch."** As a wife takes the name of her husband, so the church takes the name of Christ.

## 1. Monthly cycle and ovulation

In Leviticus 23, God gave Israel seven feasts, the first of which was Passover. It was the fourteenth day of the first month (Abib). This was important because on average, a woman ovulates on the fourteenth day of her cycle. In Leviticus 15:19-28, a woman was unclean until the fourteenth day of her cycle. They were to abstain during that time—until the ovulation! This law gave an idea of how God is concerned about procreation.

Notice in 1 Kings 23:2 that the *Word* was read on Passover. Matthew called the *Word* the *sperma*.

Let's go to another part of the Bible and find a different picture of the same thing. Paul was being shipwrecked in a storm. There was great danger. The men on the ship *fasted* for fourteen days. They ate and were cheerful. What happened next?

> **And when they had eaten enough, they...cast out the wheat into the sea.** (Acts 27:38; emphasis added)

The matter of the wheat is noteworthy. Wheat is the seed Jesus compared the Word to in Matthew 13 when it was called *sperma*. Thus, the fast and the events following is an analogy of marriage and the instruction given in Leviticus 15.

The Passover is built around the same idea. The Bible compares marital love to wine. The bread was made of wheat which is called the *sperma*. Thus, the stage is set for a conception. Marital love with the seed on the fourteenth day, the date of ovulation. Thus, we see the elements of marriage and procreation in the Passover. Can Passover lead us to His face?

To answer this, we must remember what Jesus said. These statements can be found in a Passover Haggadah and in the Gospels.

**Blessed are you, Lord, our God, King of the universe who brings forth bread from the earth.** (Haggadah)

**Take, eat; this is my body.** (Matthew 26:26)

**And he took the cup and gave thanks...** (Matthew 2:27)

**Blessed are you, Lord, our God, King of the universe who created the fruit of the vine.** (Haggadah)

**Dink ye all of it, For this is my blood of the new testament, which is shed for the remission of sin.** (Matthew 26:27-28)

Here, Jesus compares the bread and the wine to His body and the blood. On another occasion Jesus said,

**Verily, verily, I say unto you, Except ye eat the flesh of the Son of man, and drink his blood, ye have no life in you. Whosoever eateth my flesh, and drinketh my blood, hath eternal life.** (John 6:53-54)

Thus, His flesh and blood are related to life which is in His face. Again, we see that His face is related to marriage and procreation.

In John 2:14-22, our attention turns to the temple. Our bodies are called the temple (1 Corinthians 6:19), and God, the Father, and Jesus are temples (Revelation 21:22). Thus, the temple has to be studied as a picture of the male, female, and God. We will study each of these as needed.

In the temple where God resided, there was a veil that divided the holy place and the holy of holies. Jesus died on Passover (the fourteenth), and as he did, **"The veil of the temple was rent from the top to the bottom"** (Matthew 27:51). Jesus is our great High Priest. In marital relations, a woman has one high priest who breaks her veil of flesh (with the shedding of blood also).

In the most holy place behind the veil, the ark was kept. The ark was a chest built of wood and covered with gold. It contained the Ten Commandments, Aaron's rod, and a pot of manna.

**Fed thee with manna...that he might make thee know that man doth not live by bread only but by every word that proceedeth out of the mouth of the Lord doth man live.** (Deuteronomy 8:3)

The manna is like the Word which is like the seed. Thus, the Word (*sperma*) is behind the veil which is rent with blood.

## 2. Gestation

Returning to the feasts, there seems to be a parallel between the seven feasts and the gestation of a baby. We just noted the first feast, Passover. The next important event of the calendar of feasts is Pentecost, the fiftieth day. After fifty days of gestation, a human baby begins to look human. Its nondescript appearance takes on a distinct human form. God instituted the seven feasts in Leviticus 23. Hanukkah is not that apparent since it was not listed in Leviticus 23, but it seems certain that Jesus was in Jerusalem for the feast. Hanukkah has a remarkable quality. It is held at the right time after Passover be an indication of birth.

Turn your attention to the tabernacle.

**Moreover, thou shalt make the tabernacle with ten curtains. The length of one curtain shall be eight and twenty cubits.** (Exodus 26:1-2)

The perimeter of the outer court of the tabernacle was 280 cubits. The importance of this measurement is that it reflects the gestation period for a baby—280 days; that is 10 x 28, 10 lunar months, not 9 calendar months. If we used biblical units and ideas, such as a lunar month, we could find a pattern to things. Thus, the 7 feasts and the length of the curtains on the tabernacle are related to the gestation period. It is now time for birth.

## 3. Travail and birth

In John 2:23, the account returns to the Passover. Jesus is the Passover lamb and the Alpha and the Omega.

**For even Christ our passover is sacrificed for us.** (1 Corinthians 5:7)

**I am Alpha and Omega, the beginning and the
end, the first and the last.** (Revelation 22:13)

Therefore, the Passover is a beginning and end. It is not only a picture
of ovulation being on the fourteenth, it is also a picture of birth.

Turn the story to Moses as he went to Egypt to free Israel. God turned
the water to blood and sent frogs, lice, and flies. The cattle died; men and
beasts were stricken with boils and blains. There was a great hail, swarms
of locust, and great darkness. Finally, there was the death of the firstborn as
the Passover ritual took place. Israel was told to put the *blood* of a lamb on
**"the two side posts and on the upper door post of the houses"** (Exodus
12:7). That night, all the firstborn males died where there was no blood.

Pharaoh released Israel saying, **"Rise up and get you forth from
among my people"** (Exodus 12:31). He sent them out, but he changed
his mind in Exodus 14. Pharaoh followed them, entrapping them at the
Red Sea.

Moses shouted, **"Fear ye not, stand still, and see the salvation of
the Lord"** (Exodus 14:13). At God's instruction, Moses lifted his rod and
divided the sea.

When a baby is born, there is travail, the *bloody* show occurs followed
by the *water* breaking. For this reason, Jesus said, **"Ye must be born
again"** (John 3:7). It is by the blood of Jesus that we are forgiven and then
we are baptized—blood followed by water.

Now recall that God flooded the world—it had a new birth. It was
baptized—a picture of burial and new life.

## 4. Postpartum

Then Israel proceeded to Mt. Sinai. Moses went up the mountain,
fasted for forty days (Exodus 24:15-18), and received the law (Exodus
31:18). When he came down off the mountain, he found the golden calf
and broke the tables in his anger. He then returned to the top of the
mountain, fasted for forty days more (Exodus 34:28), and received the law
again (Exodus 34). This time, he received the name of God (Exodus 34:5)
and returned with his face shining.

In these events, Israel had experienced a rebirth. In Leviticus 12:1-
5, instruction is given for abstinence for a birth—forty days for a male

(Leviticus 12:2-4) and eighty days for a female (Leviticus 12:5). Since the terms of Leviticus 12 had been fulfilled, it was time for marital relations to resume. For that reason, Moses was given the law with this timing.

**And hereby we do know that we know [ginosko] Hun, if we keep His commandments.** (1 John 2:3)

Moses had the law, and he knew God. His face was shining. He was the one who knew God face-to-face.

Many things begin to come into focus. For now, we will focus on how the fear of the Lord is acquired. The fear of the Lord is related to the commandments. This is stated many times. Deuteronomy 4:10-13 and Ecclesiastes 12:13 are just two examples.

**Let us hear the conclusion of the whole matter: Fear God and keep his commandments; for this is the whole duty of man.** (Ecclesiastes 12:13)

**The fear of the Lord is the beginning of wisdom.** (Proverbs 9:10)

**A man's wisdom makes his face to shine.** (Ecclesiastes 8:1)

Thus, the law is related to the shining of His face. Finally,

**The Lord descended in a cloud...and proclaimed the name of the Lord.** (Exodus 34:5)

**Thy name is as ointment poured forth.** (Song of Solomon 1:3)

**And wine that maketh glad the heart of man, and oil to make his face to shine, and bread which strengtheneth man's heart.** (Psalm 104:15)

Thus, Moses fasted for eighty days, knew God, and received the name of God—all a picture of marriage.

As we noted earlier, the abstinence period following a male birth is forty days. This is the background meaning in events taking forty days. It is also one of the factors involved in forty years. Again, we see a pattern revealed by using biblical units of time, forty days instead of six weeks.

Jesus was baptized first, which is a picture of death, burial, and resurrection. Then He fasted for forty days and received the power of the Spirit. It's possible that some glory came to Him at that time. Since He was a perfect man and man was created to be the image and glory of God then, He was the image and glory of God and received the wine of the Spirit.

Isaac was born, lived a single life for forty years, then married Rebekah. First Corinthians 11:7 calls woman the glory of man. Marital love is compared to wine.

When God flooded (baptized) the world, it rained for forty days before the rainbow appeared. Thus, a new world was born of water. Ezekiel 1:28 compares the rainbow to the glory of God.

| Sun | Flood | 40 | Rainbow | Glory of the sun |
|-----|-------|-----|---------|------------------|
| Jesus | Baptism | 40 | Power | Glory of God |
| Isaac | Birth | 40 | Rebekah | Glory of man |

Thus, the appearance of the rainbow and the single life of Isaac are pictures of the forty days Jesus fasted, which is a picture of the forty days after birth. As we continue, we will note that Jesus's face shone as the sun (Matthew 17; Revelation 1).

\* \* \* \* \*

In this chapter, we compared the similarity of the forty days Jesus fasted to the forty years that Isaac lived as a single man. Now let's contrast their differences. The forty days Jesus fasted is a *picture* of the period of abstinence (Leviticus 12) after the birth of a male. The forty years of Isaac, though it echoes the forty days of Leviticus 12, represents a period of maturity before marriage.

Now that Israel came through the blood and water, they will spend forty years in the wilderness before they enter the promised land—Beulah. *Beulah* means married or to be a husband. The forty years in the wilderness is forty years of maturing before entering marriage.

The face of Jesus produces a union that is like marriage, and His Word produces eternal life like the seed of man procreates physical life.

# CHAPTER 2

# THE TEMPLE IN NATURE

The heavens declare the glory of God. In them
hath he set a tabernacle for the sun. Which is
as a bridegroom coming out of his chamber.
—Psalm 19:1, 4-5 (emphasis added)

It may be that you never gave our universe even a casual consideration. Then consider just two things. First is the greatness, majesty, and the power of the God of Israel. Next, consider the awe-inspiring heavens. Given the greatness of the Author and His "blackboard," what kind of message could be found there?

In this chapter, we will parallel the structure of the tabernacle with that of the heavens. Solomon suggested this parallel in his prayer at the dedication of the temple:

But will God indeed dwell on the earth? Behold, the
heaven and heaven of heavens cannot contain thee; how
much less this house that I have builded? (1 Kings 8:27)

The orbits of the planets (with one exception) are all in the same plane. This plane contains the zodiac. The *zodiac* is a circle of twelve constellations that surround the solar system. Likewise, when Moses set up the tabernacle, the tribes were arranged in twelve camps around it.

The solar system has a distinct division between the outer planets and the inner planets. The asteroid belt lies in between. When the tabernacle was built, it had two parts—the holy place and the most holy place. The veil separated the two.

> **And, behold, the veil of the temple was rent in twain
> from the top to the bottomland the rocks rent.** (Matthew
> 27:51; emphasis added)

In the middle of the inner planets is the sun—the source of light. Visible light is one of seven types of electromagnetic waves on the spectrum—gamma rays, X-rays, ultraviolet, light, infrared, microwave, and radio.

Visible light has three primary colors—blue, yellow, red—and three secondary colors—green, orange, and violet. All of these are combine to produce white as the seventh. Visible light has wavelengths that range from *70001* to *40001*. Notice the pattern: 7, 7, 7, 4.[2]

> **For the commandment is a lamp; and the law is light.**
> (Proverbs 6:23; emphasis added)

In the middle of the holy of holies was the *ark*. The ark contained the Ten Commandments. Notice that the tenth commandment has *seven parts*.

> **Thou shalt not covet thy neighbor's house, thou shalt
> not covet thy neighbor's wife, nor his manservant, nor
> his maidservant, not his ox, nor his ass, nor anything
> that is thy neighbor's.** (Exodus 20:17)

The *fourth* commandment is *seventh* from the bottom and has *seven* parts, and it pertains to the *seventh* day.

> **Remember the sabbath day to keep it holy. Six days shalt
> thou labor and do all thy work: but the seventh day is
> the sabbath of the Lord Thy God: in it thou shalt not
> do any work, thou, nor thy son, nor thy daughter, thy
> manservant, nor thy maidservant, nor thy cattle, nor
> thy stranger that is within thy gates.** (Exodus 20:8-10)

We find 7, 7, 7, 4 also in the structure of the law. Thus, 7, 7, 7, 4 occurs in the *law* and in *light*. I conclude that the solar system is built like a temple with the *sun* being the focal point like the *ark*.

---

[2]   Å is an artificial unit of measurement that does not alter the ratio of 7 and 4.

| | |
|---|---|
| Twelve constellations | Twelve tribes |
| Outer planets | Holy place |
| Asteroid belt | Veil |
| Rocks rent (Matthew 27:51) | Veil rent |
| Inner planets | Holy of holies |
| Sun | Ark (which holds the body of Christ |
| 7, 7, 7, 4—light | 7, 7, 7, 4—law |

The Bible says that His face is like the sun, **"And his countenance was as the sun shineth in his strength"** (Revelation 1:16; emphasis added). If His face is like the sun and the sun is like the ark, then His face is like the ark too.

The block of 7, 7, and 4 is in the light and the law.[3] Added together, seven plus seven plus four is eighteen. In Jewish teaching, the number 18 means life. The Hebrew word for life, *chay*, has two letters, and the letters have a numerical value which add up to eighteen. Thus, eighteen means life, and life is in His face.

The *sun* has the appearance of being the center of two circles. One is the zodiac and one is a fuzzy band in the sky—the Milky Way.

The ark has two circles. The twelve tribes circled the tabernacle and the ark. In addition, the glory of God (like a rainbow) surrounded the ark. Later (chapter 7), we will see two circles surround the *throne*.

We will now show how the sun and the solar system has the same theme (marriage and procreation) that we found in His face. We will consider this aspect of the ark in chapters 3 and 8.

Since His face is a picture of marriage and a picture of the sun, did God put pictures of marriage and procreation in and around the sun? Pluto, the last planet, travels as far as 4.6 billion miles from the sun and as close as 2.8 billion miles. (Miles are not necessarily important as units of measure, but the proportion is constant.) There are 46 chromosomes in a cell. The menstrual cycle is 28 days. The number of meteors per day is very close to the number of sperm a man releases. The difference of

---

[3] Through four may appear with three or more sevens, these seem to be variations of the central idea —7, 7, 4.

altitude of the lowest place on earth, the Dead Sea and the highest place, Mount Everest, is twenty-three times the distance the Dead Sea is below sea level. Furthermore, if it is measured in a biblical unit, a furlong, the difference of altitude is forty-six furlongs. There are 46 chromosomes in each cell. Finally, the earth moves in space in a helix, and a baby is born making a twist like a helix.

The rainbow is a picture of the glory of God. It is round like a circle. The moon circles the earth. This is a picture of woman as the glory of man. The earth circles the sun. This pictures man as the glory of God.

To take the next step in answering this question, we must consider it in relation to another question. You may recall that an atom is built like a small solar system. Therefore, it is a temple also. It has a nucleus that is circled by electrons. The nucleus is like the sun, which is like His face. Therefore, the nucleus is like His face. Are there pictures of marriage in the atom? Yes, and the first is seen in the sun. The sun produces its energy by fusion. Two atomic nuclei fuse together. Two become one. When that fusion takes place, a particle of light (photon) is emitted. Light is like the Word of God which is like the seed of man. This is fitting because the sun is like His face which is like one flesh.

Consider another aspect of the atom as seen in uranium. It has ninety-two protons in the nucleus. Ninety-two is equal to forty-six plus forty-six. There are forty-six chromosomes in a human cell. So uranium is a picture of two people in one—that is marriage. Here we see His face in the nucleus, and we see a marriage. Nine times two is equal to eight which is equal to life.

We know that uranium can split and eject two or three neutrons. These neutrons can start a chain reaction. The splitting of an atom is a picture of a broken home. When the atom splits, it shoots out neutrons that hit other atoms and cause them to split. When a home breaks up, it shoots out influence to break others. As the atom reaction releases heat and radiation, so the breaking of homes releases anger and bitterness. If a significant number of atoms split, the situation will become critical and will produce an uncontrolled explosion. If a critical number of homes break, the society will break.

**What therefore God hath joined together let not man put asunder.** (Matthew 19:6)

Another interesting aspect is the way uranium splits. It usually splits to form krypton and barium. Care to guess how many protons there are in krypton? Thirty-six. What is important about 36?

$$1 + 2 + 3 ... + 36 = 666$$

Does that number (666) look familiar? It is the "number of the beast"— the Antichrist (Revelation 13).

The conclusion is obvious. By splitting the atom and breaking the home, society is filled with fear, anger, and bitterness. This environment empowers the Antichrist to put his mark on every person.

In chapter 1, we connected marriage and His face. Now we have connected the sun to His face, the ark, and marriage.

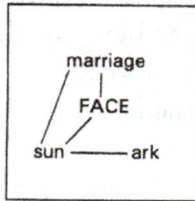

```
        marriage
           |
        FACE
       /
   sun ———— ark
```

The orbital period of the moon around the earth is the same as a woman's menstrual cycle. The number of meteors that fall to the earth per day is the same number of sperm a man releases at once. The difference of altitude of the highest place on earth—Mt. Everest—and the lowest place— the Dead Sea—is twenty-three times the distance the Dead Sea is below sea level. If this is measured in a biblical unit, the "furlong," it is a difference of forty-six furlongs. The distance of the Dead Sea and Mt. Everest is oneeighth the circumcied with the sun's motion puts the earth's trajectory in a helix, which is the same as the birth of a baby.

Let us investigate the heavens for another point of view, that is as the stars relate to our geography. First, note the North Star is above the North Pole, so it does not appear to move. Now this is a geographic and navigational convenience, but is there something more subtle? The North

Star Polaris is a triple star—three in one. So it is a clue of the Trinity God—Father, Son, and Holy Spirit. Now we saw the sign of caster and policies in relation to the Sabbath. Pollux goes precisely over Mt. Everest. It also crosses the gulf of Aqaba where the Jews crossed the sea at Nuweibaa. In one version of the Ten Commandments, it states that the commandments are to be kept in remembrance of the Exodus. Next, Pollux also crosses of the city Corpus Cristi. This is significant because Jesus called Himself the Lord of the Sabbath.

The foot of the Northern Cross goes over Mt. Everest, and the Bible says that His righteousness is like the great mountains. The foot of the Northern Cross also goes over the gulf of Aqaba at Nuweibaa. When it does, the foot of the Southern Cross goes over the northern tip of Antarctica and the northern star on the Southern Cross crosses the southern tip of South America. Three stars cross three geographic points simultaneously.

As the earth continues to rotate, the foot of the Northern Cross goes over Corpus Christi. When it does, Pollux is over Mt. Everest.

The Northern Cross and the Southern Cross are both prominent features in the Milky Way. The Bible says the heavens will roll away like a scroll. We know the Bible was written on scrolls. So let's see if there is a connection between the structure of the Milky Way and the structure of the Bible. In my opinion, this subject is so complex that a book could be written of it but one idea will suffice for here. Let's look at the Milky Way as a giant scroll. The foot of the Northern Cross and the foot of the Southern Cross is the distance of approximately 120 degrees which is 1/3 of a circle. Take the book of Psalms. Let's look at two points in the book of Psalms which is 1/3 the length of the Psalms.

**And the heavens shall declare his righteousness.** (Psalm 50:6)

**The heaven declare his righteousness.** (Psalm 97:6)

Thus, we have two crosses in the sky in the Milky Way which speaks of the rightness of God through the sacrifice of Jesus. In the northeast section of the Northern Cross, we find a well-known beautiful nebula called the North America Nebula. It looks like North America, and it goes over the geographic middle of North America.

# CHAPTER 3

# THE ARK

**The ark of the covenant...where was the golden pot that had manna, and Aaron's rod that budded and the tables of the covenant.**—Hebrews 9:4 (emphasis added)

There is a fascinating account regarding the ark in 2 Samuel 6. King David was having it brought to Jerusalem. A man was struck dead because he touched the ark. The Bible says that David was "displeased." He was also terrified that he stopped the progress. The ark was stored at the house of Obededom. The Bible says,

**The Lord blessed Obededom, and all his household.** (2 Samuel 6:11)

Something unusual was happening, and the people were talking. Upon hearing this, David brought the ark to Jerusalem with "gladness," shouting and dancing in the street. There was great blessing when the ark was present.

In chapter 1, we compared the *face* of Jesus to the marital union. Next, we compared it to the *sun*. Then we compared the *sun* to the *ark*. Now, is it possible to relate the ark and thus the temple to a body? Revelation tells us that Jesus and God are temples. First, we will attempt to show Jesus in the temple. *Our body are temples, and we were created in His image.*

**And I saw no temple therein: for the Lord God Almighty and the Lamb are the temple of it.** (Revelation 21:22)

On the far east side of the temple, we have the *brazen altar*. It stood outside the tabernacle but inside the courtyard (Exodus 40:29). The brazen altar is analogous to the feet of Jesus.

**And his [Jesus] feet like unto fine brass as if they burned in a furnace.** (Revelation 1:15; emphasis added)

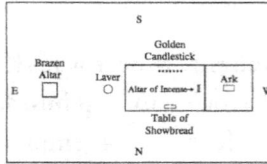

On the south side, we see that the golden candlestick with seven candles (Exodus 40:24). A reference to the candlestick is also found in Revelation. If the temple pictures Jesus with His back on the ground, then the south side of the temple corresponds to His right hand.

**"And he had in this right hand seven stars:...and his countenance was as the sun shineth in his strength."** (Revelation 1:16)

Thus, the brazen altar and the golden candlestick are consistent with each other.

It appears that His face would be in the ark. Is this consistent with what we have discussed? The reader will recall that the face of Jesus was compared to the sun (Matthew 17:2; Revelation 1:16). In chapter 3, we saw that the solar system is a temple with the sun analogous to the ark. Since the face of Jesus is like the sun and the sun is like the ark, it follows that His face must relate to the ark. It is consistent with our previous ideas, so let us look closer at this.

According to Hebrews 9:4, the ark contained a golden pot of *manna*, *Aaron S rod*, and the two *stones* that had the Ten Commandments.

Manna was compared to God's Word in Deuteronomy 8:3. Thus, the manna is in the right place—in the ark.

**Keep my commandments and live; and my law as the apple of thine eye.** (Proverbs 7:2; emphasis added)

Notice that Proverbs 7:2 connects the law and the eyes. Next, the Scripture calls both a light. The eye is a light, and the law is a light. It seems they are related.

**The light of the body is the eye.** (Matthew 6:2)

**And the law is light.** (Proverbs 6:23; emphasis added)

It appears that the two stones are like two eyes. Then the contents—the two stones (eyes), Aaron's rod (nose), and the pot of manna (Word from God's mouth)—resemble a *face*. Thus, it seems that we have found Jesus in the tabernacle.

At this point, we need to comment on the humanity of Christ. The eyes see the seven colors in the spectrum of light. The nose can detect seven types of smell—camphoraceous, ethereal, floral, musk, peppermint, pungent, and putrid. Finally, the tongue has four types of taste—sweet, sour, bitter, and salt. Seven, seven, and four add up to eighteen. Eighteen is the number for life, and life is in the face of the king.

**What? know ye not that your body is the temple of the Holy Ghost which is in you, which ye have of God, and ye are not your own?** (1 Corinthians 6:19)

It is time to think about the ark in regard to our humanity. In the case of man, there is a difference. We know the manna is compared to the Word of God and that in Matthew 13, the Word is called the *sperma*. Since the manna is like the seed of man, it appears that Aaron's rod and the two stones are a male symbol.

The ark and its contents take on a different meaning. When the temple is human instead of divine, the body reverses direction. The head is on the east end instead of the west though the holy of holies stays in the west. The Word of God is like the seed of man—it creates life.

Next, we see the parallel of Genesis 3:21—the disappearance of God's face and the clothing of Adam and Eve.

In chapter 1, we connected marriage and His face. In chapter 2, we connected the sun to His face and the ark. Now we have connected the ark to His face and to marriage.

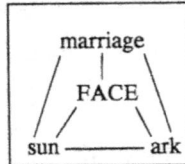

```
         marriage
          |
     /   FACE   \
    /      |      \
  sun ——————— ark
```

\* \* \* \* \*

An interesting coincidence?

When reading about the construction of the tabernacle, the reader will see that the ark was in the most holy place. It was ten cubits by ten cubits by ten cubits in size. The holy place was ten cubits by ten cubits by twenty cubits in size. The ark was in the middle of the most holy place; it was five cubits from the west wall and twenty-five cubits from the entrance at the first veil. The ark's position divided the length of the tabernacle into five cubits and twenty-five cubits or into one-sixth and five sixth. That was the exact location of the ark, the law, Aaron's rod, and the pot of manna.

We saw how our solar system was designed as a temple. Let us take this idea a bit further. Where are we located in the Milky Way galaxy? Are we near the middle? Or some far fringe? Well, we are one-sixth of the total length from the end, just like the ark! And there is a veil of gas and dust between us and the center of the galaxy.

Try another example. Hold your Bible and find the total number of pages. Divide it by six and you will find Moses receiving the Ten Commandments in Deuteronomy 5, one-sixth of the way through the Bible.

In the New Testament, locate Mark 7. These scriptures speak of the commandments and cup. They are one-sixth of the way through the New Testament.

Finally, the location of the temple of Israel was one-sixth of the circumference of the earth from the North Pole.

Thus, the ark is one-sixth of the length of the temple from the west wall. The temple in Israel was one-sixth of the circumference of the earth from the North Pole. The earth is one-sixth of the length of the galaxy from the edge.

# CHAPTER 4

# TITHE

# PART 1

In this chapter, we are going to show the practical results of chapter 1. There are two elements that are like "twins" that they seem so close—the tithe and the commandments. Note that there are Ten Commandments and the tithe is one-tenth.

The scriptures relate each of these elements to the *eyes*. First,

**He that hasteth to be rich hath an evil eye and considereth not that poverty shall come upon him.** (Proverbs 28:22)

Next,

**Keep my commandment and live and my law as the apple of thine eye.** (Proverbs 7:2)

In chapter 1, the *commandments* were related to the *fear of God*. This is true also of the *tithe*. This chapter shows much of the practical application of this study. It also hints at the great interrelationship of everything.

**Thou shall truly tithe all the increase of thy seed... The tithe of the corn, of thy wine and of thine oil, and the firstlings of thy herds and of thy flocks; that thou mayest learn to fear the Lord thy God always.** (Deuteronomy 14:2223; emphasis added)

Thus, the tithe, like the commandments, is related to the fear of God, which is related to wisdom, which makes a man's face to shine. Thus, the tithe brings us to His face and back to procreation and salvation.

Let us begin by noting some results of the tithe.

> **Bring ye all the tithes into the storehouse. And I will rebuke the devourer for your sakes and he shall not destroy the fruits of your ground, neither shall your vine cast her fruit before the time in the field saith the Lord of hosts. (Malachi 3:10-11)**

\* \* \* \* \*

*There are seven two-part principles that come from the promise.*

1.  Tithing protects finances; greed opens the way for the thief.

The first application of Malachi 3:10-11 refers to economics. This verse was addressed to an agricultural society. If the fruit of their ground and vines was productive, they prospered. If not, they had a lack. Malachi 3 states that God would bless His people if they tithed. Jesus said,

> **The thief cometh not, but for to steal, and to kill and to destroy.** (John 10:10; emphasis added)

The presence or absence of tithing either opens or shuts the door to the thief.

## Seed of man

2.  Tithing protects the unborn (and children); greed gives place to the destroyer.

> **Neither shall your vine cast her fruit...** (Malachi 3:11; emphasis added)

**Thy wife shall be as a fruitful vine.** (Psalm 128:3; emphasis added)

**Lo, children are an heritage of the Lord and the fruit of the womb is his reward.** (Psalm 127:3; emphasis added)

We discover that the wife is a vine and children are the fruit of the vine. If we connect this to Malachi 3, we see that the tithe protects the fruit (children) of the vine (wife). The lack of tithing causes the loss of fruit. Why are we losing our families and children? Why are we seeing such great losses through drugs, alcohol, and suicide? Why are we seeing such loss through abortion? The tithe!

**The thief cometh not, but for to steal, and to kill and to destroy.** (John 10:10)

3. Having children is a financial blessing; birth control is a financial curse.

Alabama senator, Jeremiah A. Denton, said, "The family is the engine that drives civilization. Throughout history, those cultures that have failed to found their rules and attitudes of society on the central importance of the family unit have decayed and disintegrated."

**Praise ye the Lord. Blessed is the man that feareth the Lord, that delighteth greatly in his commandments.
His seed shall be mighty upon earth.
Wealth and riches shall be in his house.**
(Psalm 112:1, 3; emphasis added)

Notice the threefold appearance of the fear of God, children, and prosperity. This occurs at least four times in the Bible. Hence, it is not a coincidence. These three factors interweave and depend upon each other.

In Exodus 1:15-21 (emphasis added), we find the story of an attempt to kill the coming deliverer. A slaughter of male babies was ordered—**"But the midwives feared God"** and **"saved the men children alive"** and

**"and it came to pass because the midwives feared God, that he made them houses."**

God gave a blessing to them for their actions.

The same pattern occurs in Job 1:1-3. He feared God, had ten children, and had so much substance that **"this man was the greatest of all the men of the east."**

Genesis 1:28 commands: **"Be fruitful and multiply."** If all the people of the world were standing together with one square yard per person, the whole human race would occupy a square area of forty miles times forty miles. The population explosion is a myth.

Actually, the opposite is true. We are experiencing a birth shortage of crisis proportions. If things continue as they are in America, in a few decades, we will be faced with having two to three working people for each retired person! How will we afford it?

In chapter 1, we paralleled marriage with Christ and the church and procreation with the new birth. The next two principles logically parallel the last two.

## *Word of God*

4. Tithing protects unborn souls; love of money aborts souls.

In John 15:4, Jesus stated, **"I am the vine, ye are the branches (emphasis added)."** The tithe applies to a literal vine, the wife, and now, *Jesus*. As the lack of tithing aborts the fruit of the vine and wife, so we lose the fruit of new souls.

**"The thief comes not, but for to steal, and to kill and to destroy (emphasis added)."** This is the result of taking God's tithe. The devil robs us of the money we robbed from God (Malachi 3). He kills literally and finally causes souls to have body and soul destroyed in hell.

5. Leading people to Christ brings financial blessing; ignoring souls brings a curse.

In Matthew 16:26, Jesus states, **"For what is a man profited, if he shall gain the whole world and lose his own soul?"** Thus, there is material value and spiritual value. Different yet similar. We can see that the way God purifies His people is similar to the way silver is refined.

**The words of the Lord are pure words; as silver tried in a furnace of earth purified seven times.** (Psalm 12:6)

Parallel this verse with these three verses:

**Seeing ye have purified your souls.** (1 Peter 1:21)

**Beloved, think it not strange concerning the fiery trial which is to try you.** (1 Peter 4:12)

**For a just man falleth seven times and riseth up again.** (Proverbs 24:16)

Thus, there is a parallel of treatment of souls (spiritual value) and silver (economic value). Any parallel that God places in His creations means that these probably, if not always, impact each other.

**The just seek his soul.** (Proverbs 29:10; emphasis added)

What are we *seeking*? The Bible tells us what to seek.

**My soul if thou wilt receive my word and hide my commandments with thee.**

**So that thou incline thine ear unto wisdom and apply thine heart to understanding.**

**Yea, if thou criest after knowledge...**

**If thou seek her as silver.** (Proverbs 2:1-4)

We are to seek souls and wisdom. And note that He said to seek wisdom as silver. Proverbs 11:30 states, **"He that wins souls is wise"** and

Proverbs 14:24 says, **"The crown of the wise is their riches."** Thus, true prosperity is related to evangelism.

## Word and seed

6. Tithing protects Israel; love of money aborts the fruit.

> **For the vineyard of the Lord of host is the house of Israel.**
> (Isaiah 5:7)

Thus, Israel is the third vine that loses its fruit from greed.

7. Helping Israel brings financial blessing; hurting Israel brings a curse.

> **And I will bless them that bless thee, and curse them that curseth thee.** (Genesis 12:3)

Here we see God's promise for those who bless Israel.

\* \* \* \* \*

In closing, notice that these seven laws are grouped in three pairs. This pattern of three pairs and a single will return. In response to the tithe, God promises to protect the fruit of your vine(s) economically, the fruit of your wife, the fruit of souls, and the fruit of Israel.

Now we know that the tithe affects the fruit of the vine. If the grapes are lost, so is the wine. And what did we find the wine to be? It is marital love (Song of Solomon 1), the blood (Matthew 26:28), and the spirit (Acts 2:4). We lose the joy of marriage and salvation.

# PART 2

Part 2 of this chapter is as practical as part 1, but first, it connects other parts of the book.

> **He that Is greedy of gain troubleth his own house, but he that hateth gifts shall live.** (Proverbs 15:27; emphasis added)

Greed brings a house trouble. This verse has several applications as follows:

1. Greed will disrupt your home. It can ruin a marriage. It can destroy every part of a home.
2. The temple is called a house. And greed can destroy a church. It is a sad reality that most churches are totally dysfunctional because of the power of money.
3. The human body is called a temple. Greed can trouble your body. Many people today have troubled bodies—ulcers, migraines, etc. — from the love of money.
4. In chapter 3, we showed that the solar system is a temple (and thus a house). There are some scriptures that show that the earth will be plagued even from the heavens.

**He that troubleth his own house shall inherit the wind.**
(Proverbs 11:29; emphasis added)
The wind brings another set of curses compatible to a troubled house.

1. The first wind is an angry woman. Lack of tithing will cause trouble with angry women. The woman can be literal or figurative.

**A continual dropping in a very rainy day and a contentious woman are alike.**

**Whosoever hideth her hideth the wind.** (Proverbs 27:15
16; emphasis added)

2. The next wind you can experience is the wind of deception and doctrine.

**That we hence forth be no more children, tossed to and fro, and carried about with every wind of doctrine.**
(Ephesians 4:14)

3. Another possible wind is the solar wind. I believe that we are going to experience great problems from the sun.

**And the fourth angel poured out his vial upon the sun; and power was given unto him to scorch men with fire.** (Revelation 16:8)

It may seem that this section has simply fired in several directions. That is because the tithe is connected to His face, and His face is everywhere. Hence, the influence of the tithe is everywhere.

## CHAPTER 5

# GEOGRAPHY

**Hear, O Israel: The Lord our God is one Lord.**[4]
—Deuteronomy 6:4

The word *hear* (*shema* in Hebrew) is an important one in Jewish life and culture. In Judaism, Deuteronomy 6:4 is called the *shema*. It is the watchword of Judaism. It is the first complete sentence that a Jew learns. The observant Jew speaks it every evening and morning for the whole of his life. It is to be the last thing he says in departing life. Thus, it is reasonable that God create a picture dealing with this subject.

If you look at a globe, you will notice that Israel is very small and it is placed in an area so that it looks like an eardrum. The Mediterranean Sea would be like the ear canal. The Red Sea is like the eustachian tube. The Word of God is to be heard.

In Acts 27, Paul had a troubled voyage to Rome as he sailed in the Mediterranean Sea. Then they **"cast out the wheat into the Sea"** (Acts 27:38). We know that Jesus compared the Word of God to wheat. Thus, this is consistent with our previous comments of the Mediterranean. This is a picture of the Word entering the ear canal. When Paul was shipwrecked, healings and miracles occurred. People responded to the Gospel.

What is the Word of God like? It is like the seed of man. Is Israel also like the womb of the earth? Is there a picture of a baby here? If we return to the passage in Acts 27, we find that they had been fasting for fourteen days.

---

[4]  The Hebrew word for one is echad. It is plural and masculine. Since it is plural, it suggests that God has a plurality in His being, in one.

**This day is the fourteenth day that ye have tarried and continued fasting.** (Acts 27:33)

Recall that in Leviticus 15, a woman is unclean until the fourteenth day of her cycle. The events of Acts 27 tell a picture of Leviticus 15. Jesus compared the wheat to the seed of man, calling it the *sperma*. The ovulation is the fourteenth. Thus, the scene is set for new life. It seems that the Sea of Galilee is a picture of a placenta. The Jordan River is like an umbilical cord. The Dead Sea is a picture of a baby.

Furthermore, the Dead Sea is 1,312 feet below sea level. Mt. Everest is 29,028 feet above sea level, which places it 30,040 feet above the Dead Sea. That difference is 23 times the 1,312. There are 23 chromosomes in a sperm cell. The sperm is like the wheat which is like the Word.

In addition, there is a star, Pollux, which the Bible calls a sign (Acts 28:11). It is the twenty-third brightest night time object when you include the moon and the planets. It passes exactly over Mt. Everest.

Thus, this is another parallel of the Word of God and the seed of man, of birth, and the new birth.

\* \* \* \* \*

There are some important practical applications of this information. They are related to our sense of balance or equilibrium. The ear is important to our equilibrium.

When we abort the Word of God, we lose our equilibrium. Indeed, we have done this. We have demolished our entire social structure. We refused to hear God's Word, and we reaped havoc.

We need to be very careful to be fair and just toward Israel. If not, we can rupture the equilibrium of the world.

Lastly, we will experience more trouble as we abort man's seed.

## CHAPTER 6

# MAZZAROTH[5]

In this chapter, we will do two things. First, develop a few of the previous ideas; and two, set the scene for future chapters.

We saw how the solar system was a picture of the temple. Then we found a bigger temple—the galaxy. Its veil is the clouds of dust and gas that hides our view of the center of the galaxy. For this reason, we found the Ten Commandments also in the zodiac, in addition to the seven days of creation and the twelve sons of Israel.

- Temple
- Veil
- Commandments
- Galaxy
- Clouds of gas/dust
- Zodiac

Thus, we find a bigger temple (galaxy) which encloses the smaller temple of the solar system. This expanded repetition then transforms the zodiac from the twelve tribes that surround the tabernacle to the Ten Commandments in the ark in the most holy place.

**Wherefore the children of Israel shall keep the sabbath, to observe the sabbath through their generations, for a perpetual covenant. It is a sign between me and the children of Israel forever; for in six days the Lord made heaven and earth, and on the seventh day He rested and was refreshed.**

(Exodus 31:16-17)

We will find this sign playing a very beautiful role in our marriage picture; but first, we need some interesting background. The Sabbath is the fourth commandment.

If you read Genesis, you will find an interesting pattern. Any idea that God begins to work on, He finishes three days later. On the first day, God said, **"Let there be light."**

On the fourth day, He said, **"Let there be lights in the firmament of the heaven"** (Genesis 1:3, 14). On the fourth day, God made the sun and the moon. (The lunar period is twenty-eight days.) This pattern is found also in the second and fifth days and the third and sixth—that is three pairs. And the Sabbath is the seventh day, **"He rested on the seventh day"** (Genesis 2:2).

What is His face like? The sun. Thus, we find His face suggested in the fourth day.

The same pattern exists in the Ten Commandments, except the order is reversed (remember how the temple was reversed in chapter 4). The last commandment states, **"Thou shalt not covet thy neighbor's wife"** (Exodus 20:17).

Exodus 20:14 says, **"Thou shalt not commit adultery,"** three laws earlier. (The woman's period is twenty-eight days.) And each of the last six commandments has a pair. So the last six commandments make three pairs too! With the Sabbath on top, seventh from the bottom.

> **Remember the sabbath day to keep it holy.** (Exodus 20:8)

What is His face like? Marriage. His face is suggested in the seventh commandment.

## Seven days of creation

7 Sabbath

6

5

4 Let there be lights (sun, moon)

3
4
1 Let there be light
*Last seven commandments*
Remember the Sabbath 4
5
6
7 Thou shall not commit adultery
8
9
10 Thou shall not covet neighbor's wife

Since the seven days of creation is parallel and therefore anticipate the last seven commandments, we will see that the creation week and the law is in the zodiac.

**Whose sign was Castor and Pollux.** (Acts 28:11)

Castor and Pollux are called signs. Since the Sabbath is a sign, then is the Sabbath related to Castor and Pollux?

Castor and Pollux are the two brightest stars in the constellation Gemini. Gemini is the fourth constellation of the zodiac. The Sabbath is the fourth commandment. So it seems there is a parallel here. The zodiac starts at Pisces because that is where it crosses the earth's equator.

Our sun is a single star. Castor is not. It is a triple star! Three stars in orbit together. And each of these three is a double star! Castor is six stars in one, three pairs. Does this sound familiar? And Pollux is the seventh—the Sabbath. Let us look closer.

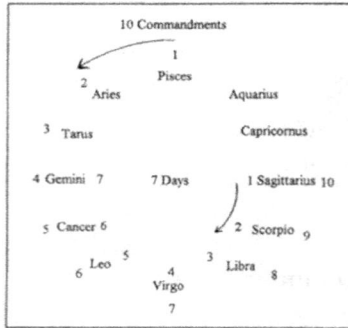

Count all the stars brighter than Castor but fainter than Pollux. This is the group increasing in brightness—twenty-third, *Castor*; twenty-second, Adhara; twenty-first, Regulus; twentieth, Beta Crucis; nineteenth, Deneb; eighteenth, Fomalhaut; seventeenth, *Pollux*—the Sabbath. Castor is the twenty-third brightest star in the sky; Pollux is the seventeenth. Observe the five stars between Castor and Pollux. That makes a list of seven—with Castor as the dimmest of the seven and Pollux as the brightest! So here is a picture of the six days God worked and the Sabbath.

How does the brightness of Castor and Pollux rank in the zodiac? In the zodiac, Pollux is the fourth brightest. Castor ranks seventh in the zodiac. So here is another picture of the Sabbath, the fourth commandment and the seventh day. There are just two stars in the zodiac in order of brightness between Castor and Pollux—Fomalhaut and Regulus.

There is one more thing we must consider. If we look for the nucleus of our galaxy, we will find it in Sagittarius. I would say that is a *light*. If we advance around the zodiac three places, we come to Virgo. Virgo is famous for being the location of a cluster of two thousand to three thousand galaxies. Is that *lights*? If we proceed another three places around the zodiac, we land at *Gemini* (seventh from Sagittarius). The *sign* of Castor and Pollux are in Gemini.

In Sagittarius, Virgo, and Gemini, we find a picture of Genesis 1. The first day: **"Let there be light,"** the fourth day: **"Let there be lights,"** and the seventh day: **"He rested on the seventh day."**

Since the seven days of creation parallel to the seven of the Ten Commandments, we have also a picture of the Ten Commandments in the zodiac. That makes the zodiac part of a bigger ark of a bigger temple—the galaxy.

**The heavens declare his righteousness...** (Psalm 97:6)

There is another interesting facet to Sagittarius, Virgo, and Gemini. Here we find the patriarchs of Israel. Sagittarius is where the nucleus of our galaxy is located. The nucleus represents Abraham since his seed is like the stars.

> **Look now toward heaven, and tell the stars, if thou be able to number them: and he said unto him, So shall thy seed be.** (Genesis 15:5)

Gemini is the constellation that has the twins; therefore, it is a picture of the twins, Esau and Jacob.

Between Sagittarius and Gemini is Virgo, and between Abraham and Jacob is Isaac. Virgo represents a virgin; Christ was born of a virgin. Isaac also had a miraculous conception since Sarah was too old. Jesus died as the Passover lamb. Isaac foreshadowed this on Mount Mariah with Abraham, his father. Thus, he is a type of Christ but so is the ram that died in his place.

As we noted, Virgo contains a cluster of galaxies. It is about sixty-five million light years from here.

> **That one day is with the Lord as a thousand years, and a thousand years as one day.** (2 Peter 3:8)

If you convert 65 million years according to this ratio, the corresponding time is 180 years.

> **And the days of Isaac were an hundred and fourscore years...and died.** (Genesis 35:28-29)

Furthermore, recall that Hebrew letters and words have numerical value. The letters of the word for *face (paniym)* add up to 180. Thus, 180 take us to a face and to Isaac, a type of Christ.

In the zodiac, we find the twelve tribes of Israel. Since Jesus's face is like the ark and the sun, then the zodiac also represents the twelve apostles. We found Abraham, Isaac, and Jacob in the zodiac. It also has the Ten Commandments and the seven days of the week. And since it has the commandments, the zodiac is the contents of a bigger ark of a bigger temple—the galaxy.

Seeing we have looked at the tithe and the Sabbath, there is something very interesting under the surface. That is they are both connected to time, and God makes specific requirements of each. The Sabbath is one-seventh of the week, and the tithe is one-tenth the income. Since both of these speak to requirements on our time, let's add them. One-seventh plus one-tenth times six sevenths come out to 23 percent.

---

5  *Mazzaroth* is the Hebrew word used for the *zodiac* in Job 38:32.

# CHAPTER 7

# REVIVAL

T o address the topic of revival, we must revisit and continue discussion of the tithe and the commandments.

These topics have a close association—both produce the fear of God. When there is fear of the Lord, the stage is set for revival.

> **Bring ye all the tithes into the storehouse, that there may be meat in mine house, and prove me now herewith, saith the Lord of hosts if I will not open you the windows of heaven, and pour you out a blessing that there shall not be room enough to receive it. And, I will rebuke the devourer for your sakes and he shall not destroy the fruits of your ground.** (Malachi 3:10-11)

In only one other place in the Bible did God speak of opening the windows of heaven on the occasion of the flood (Genesis 7:11).

> **And it shall come to pass, if ye shall harken diligently unto my commandments which I command you this day.**

> **That I will give you the rain of your land in his due season, the first rain and the latter rain.** (Deuteronomy 11:13-14; emphasis added)

The rain results from the *tithe* and the *commandments*.

Commandments
Rain
Tithe

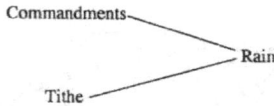

On many occasions, the Bible mentions a cloud. When Moses built the tabernacle, the cloud containing the presence of God appeared (Exodus 40:35). When Solomon built the temple (1 King 8:11), the cloud resided in it. Jesus left the earth in a cloud, and in Luke 21:27, we find, **"And then shall they see the Son of man coming in a cloud with power and great glory."**

**The Lord rides on a swift cloud.** (Isaiah 19:1)

God's presence and power are found in a cloud.

**And suddenly there came a sound from heaven as of a rushing mighty wind.** (Acts 2:2)

**The wind bloweth where it listed.** (John 3:8)

We find the presence of the Spirit moves like a great wind.

**Then shall we know if we follow on to know the Lord; his going forth is prepared as the morning and he shall come unto us as the rain, as the latter and former rain unto the earth.**[6] (Hosea 6:3; emphasis added)

The Hebrew word used here for *know* is also used in regard to marriage, **"And Adam knew Eve his wife; and she conceived..."** (Genesis 4:1; emphasis added). There we find our familiar theme. The Word, which is like the seed of man, is compared to water. Yet Hosea is speaking of the kingdom of God, and he is saying that God will come to us as the rain.

---

[6] The molecular weight of water is 18, the number for life. Life eternal is to know God and His Son.

The rain is like the Spirit and the Word. Jesus said to the adulteress that He was able to give **"a well of water springing up unto eternal life"** (John 4:14).

Paul said that, **"He [Christ] might sanctify and cleanse it [the church] with the washing of the water by the word"** (Ephesians 5:26).

Thus, we see the Word and Spirit liken to water. It is able to cleanse us by washing, to quench thirst, and to be contained in wells, and it is able to flow.

> **Whosoever drinketh of this water shall thirst again; but whosoever drinketh of the water that I shall given him shall never thirst, but the water that I shall give him shall be in him a well of water springing up unto everlasting life.** (John 4:13-14)

> **If any man thirst, let him come unto me and drink. He that believeth on me, as the Scripture hath said, out of his belly shall flow rivers of living waters.** (John 8:37-38)

When it rains, the water soaks into the soil to sustain the life and some flows into brooks, streams, and rivers, so it is in the Spirit.

*First, it flows into the brooks, so it is in the Spirit.*

> **The words of a man's mouth is the wellspring of wisdom as a flowing brook.** (Proverbs 18:7; emphasis added)

Next, the brooks merge to form streams.

> **But let judgement run down like waters and righteousness as a mighty stream.** (Amos 5:24; emphasis added)

Then the streams join to form rivers.

> **Thou shalt make them drink of the river of thy pleasures.** (Psalm 36:8; emphasis added)

**O, that thou hadst harkened to my commandments then
had thy peace been as a river.** (Isaiah 48:18; emphasis added)

**But ye shall receive power [dunamis] after the Holy
Ghost is come upon you.** (Acts 1:8)

The power of the Spirit is like lightning or electricity. It abides in the
cloud and is given to His people.

**And his strength is in the clouds...die God of Israel
is he that giveth strength and power unto his people.**
(Psalm 68:34-35)

## Lightning power

Wherever there is lightning, there is thunder. And God's voice is like
thunder.

**God thundereth marvelously with his voice.** (Job 37:5)

Lighting Power
Thunder Voice
Light Word

**Where the word of the king is, there is power.**
(Ecclesiastes 8:4)

In chapter 2, we noted that the tithe and commandments were
necessary for rain and for the fear of God. Recall that **"the fear of the
Lord is the beginning of wisdom"** and **"a man's wisdom maketh his
face to shine"** (Ecclesiastes 8:1).

Jesus's face "was as the sun shineth in his strength [dunimis]"
(Revelation 1:16).

```
                    ┌── Tithe ──┐
Rain ──<            >── Fear of God  →Wisdom  →Face
        └ Commandments ┘
```

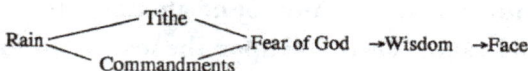

When the sun appears during rain, it produces a rainbow, so with the face of Jesus. The Bible compares the glory of God to being like a rainbow.

> **As the appearance of the bow that is in the cloud in the day of rain, so was the appearance of the brightness round about. This was the appearance of the likeness of the glory of the Lord.** (Ezekiel 1:28)

*The Face*

The rainbow results from the light passing through the water. Water is like the knowledge of the glory of God.

> **For the earth shall be filled with the knowledge of the glory of the Lord, as the waters cover the sea.** (Habakkuk 2:14)

The light that passes through the water to mate a rainbow comes from the sun. The light is from the sun. The sun is like the face of Jesus, which radiates the light of the knowledge of the glory of God.

> **For God who commanded the light to shine out of darkness, hath shined in our hearts, to given the light of the knowledge of the glory of God in the face of Jesus Christ.** (2 Corinthians 4:6)

*The Face*

Revelation 1:16 is sun face of Jesus.
Second Corinthians 4:6 is the light of the knowledge of the glory of God.
Habakkuk 2:14 is the water knowledge of the glory of God.
Ezekiel 1:28 is the rainbow glory of God.
We can find a picture of this in Revelation.

> **And immediately I was in the Spirit and behold a throne was set in heaven and one sat on the throne. And he that sat was to look upon like a jasper and sardine stone, and there was a rainbow round about the throne in sight**

**like unto an emerald. And round about the throne were four and twenty seats and upon the seats I saw four and twenty elders sitting. And out of the throne proceedeth lightnings and thunderings.** (Revelation 4:2-5; emphasis added)

Whenever the Bible speaks of an *archer S bow*, it uses the same Hebrew word as it does for *rainbow*. And the Bible compares *lightning* to an *arrow*.

**Yea, he sent out his arrows, and scattered them, and he shot out lightning, and discomfited them.** (Psalm 18:14)

God's glory and power is His bow and arrow. And how we need this! It is His way of deliverance. Is there a way to obtain this kind of revival? And deliverance? Yes, it comes from tithing and keeping the commandments, repentance and prayer, and even fasting. But there is another necessary factor.

Remember what we discovered about His face in chapter 1? It is the key to the marital parallel of Ephesians 5:32. Thus, what we see around His face mirrors things in the home.

What is the glory of man? Woman.

**For a man indeed ought not to cover his head, forasmuch as he is the image and glory of God, but the woman is the glory of man.** (1 Corinthians 11:7)

What are the arrows of man? Children.

**As arrows are in the hand of a mighty man, so are children of the youth. Happy is the man that hath his quiver full of them.** (Psalm 127:4-5; emphasis added)

A man's glory and power is his wife and children—his bow and arrows.

**Out of the mouth of babes and sucklings hast thou ordained strength because of thine enemies, that thou mightest still the enemy and the avenger.** (Psalm 8:2)

What is happening to America? We are throwing our arrows away. It does not matter whether you are a pacifist or not; the disarmament of our country does not mean world peace. It means that we deserve no protection since we reject the arrows God gives. God is removing the "arrows" we make. This is part of the judgment that is beginning.

We think of lightning and thunder perhaps separately, but remember they happen at the same time. The *thunder* is like God's voice, and God's Word is light. Lightning flashes are arrows, and children are arrows.

**Thy word...is a light unto my path...(Psalm 119:105)**

Nature has a picture of revival—a thunderstorm. This parable has another parallel built in. We saw that God and man have glory and power that is pictured as a bow and arrow. Thus, if we are to have revival, we must do something that was not required of the previous generation because they did not have a great lack of children. So we must "build the old waste places" (Isaiah 58:12) and add on from there. Think about what Jesus said:

**And whoso shall receive one such little child in my name receives me.** (Matthew 18:5)

**And he that receiveth me receiveth Him that sent me.** (Matthew 10:14)

Is this not amazing? If we reject children, we reject Christ! If we reject Christ, we reject the Father! Will we reject the Father to receive the thief? We started this chapter with the tithe.

**Bring ye all the tithes into the storehouse.and I will rebuke the devourer.**

**And he shall not destroy the fruit of your ground, neither shall your vine cast her fruit before the time in the field.** (Malachi 3:10-11)

**The thief cometh not, but for to steal and to kill, and to destroy. I am come that they might have life, and that they might have it more abundantly.** (John 10:10)

# CHAPTER 8

# THE SIGNS

# PART 1

There are many things in the Bible called a sign. Most, if not all of them, can be harmonized into one picture, connecting the death and resurrection of Christ. A study of the signs will show that the death and resurrection of Christ is a picture of marriage and conception. Sometimes a thing is called a token, but the word used for *token* is the same Hebrew word as used for a *sign* (*owth*).

If the Passover is a remembrance of the Exodus, could there be something in the Passover that relates to the signs? As a matter of fact, it appears that the whole set of plagues were signs.

**And I will harden Pharaoh's heart, and will multiply my signs in the land of Egypt.** (Exodus 7:3)

**Behold, I will set swarms of flies...I will put a division between my people and thy people; tomorrow shall this sign be.** (Exodus 8:21, 23)

**And the Lord said unto Moses, Go in unto Pharaoh: for I have hardened his heart, that I Might show these my signs before him.** (Exodus 10:1)

**And Moses said unto the people, Remember this day [Passover] in which ye came out of Egypt.there shall no leaven be eaten.**

**And it shall be a sign unto thee...** (Exodus 13:3, 9)

The plagues of Egypt that preceded the Exodus are a picture of travail and are signs. They related to other signs in a picture of marriage and procreation. They are the travail that proceeds birth, and birth is also the picture in the Passover.

Notice that the sun and moon are signs.

> **And God said, Let there be light in the firmament of heaven...and let them be for signs.**

> **And God made two great lights. The greater light to rule the day, and the lesser light to rule the night.** (Genesis 1:14, 16)

The sun and moon were made signs on the fourth day of creation. It was on the fourth day when the sun darkened as Jesus gave up His life on the cross.

> **Now from the sixth hour there was darkness over the land unto the ninth hour.** (Matthew 27:45)

Since the sun darkened and His face is like the sun, did something happen to His face?

> **As many were astonished at thee, his visage was so marred more than any man, and his form more than the sons of men.**

(Isaiah 52:14)

Since something happened to the sun and His face, did something happen that can give us a picture of marriage and children? It seems that a study of signs will take us from a virgin to a baby.

> **Therefore the Lord himself shall give you a sign, behold a virgin shall conceive, and bear a son, and shall call his name Immanuel.** (Isaiah 7:14; emphasis added)

The Messiah was to be born of a virgin by the Word of God, and this is the fulfillment of the prophecy.

There is another reason why this event was called a sign. The blood of Jesus is a picture of the blood of a virgin. To understand the importance of this sign, it must be viewed with other signs.

> **And the blood shall be to you for a token [sign].** (Exodus 12:13)

> **And the Lord said unto Moses, bring Aaron's rod again before the testimony, to be kept for a token [sign] against the rebels.** (Numbers 17:10)

Recall in chapter 4 that Aaron's rod was in the ark with the tables of the covenant and the pot of manna. We saw that Aaron's rod is a male symbol. The manna is like the Word of God which is like the seed of man. As we study the signs and the death of Christ, something happens—the male and female become one. The rod is masculine. The veil and blood are female.

When Jesus was dying, **"the veil of the temple was rent in twain from the top to the bottom"** (Matthew 27:51). Thus, the blood is the sign of the Messiah, the lamb without spot, and the sign of a virgin (Deuteronomy 22:15).

All these pieces belong together. In the ark was Aaron's rod and the manna. Here is the marriage of a virgin. Recall the bread (wheat is the *sperma*) and the wine (thy love is better than wine) on the fourteenth—the ovulation. Jesus died on Passover, the fourteenth day of Abib. The stage is set for new life.

\* \* \* \* \*

Let's move on to a new idea related to the sign of Jonah. This will lead us to the new life in conception and resurrection.

**For as Jonah was three days and three nights in the whale's belly, so shall the Son of Man be three days and three nights in the heart of the earth.** (Matthew 12:40)

While we will not discuss this for great length, we must mention it, and we will examine it as literal.

The first thing that is apparent is that it is not three days and three nights from Friday night to Sunday morning. Since Jesus died and was buried around sunset, the lapse of three full days brings us to another sunset. He was alive on the morning of the first day.

**As it began to dawn toward the first day of the week, came Mary Magdalene and the other Mary to see the sepulchre.** (Matthew 28:1)

Therefore, He must have been resurrected around sunset on the Sabbath. For additional study, read John 19:31, Mark 16:1, and Luke 23:56. I believe that a study of the resurrection reveals that it was not by chance that in creation (Genesis 1), God always took three days to finish one idea.

If this was so, then the sign of Jonah started with a Passover Sabbath (Leviticus 23:6-7) and ended with the weekly Sabbath—which is a sign.

**Wherefore the children of Israel shall keep the sabbath, to observe the sabbath throughout their generations, for a perpetual covenant. It is a sign between me and the children of Israel for ever...** (Exodus 31:16-17)

Recall in chapter 6 that the sign of the Sabbath was related to the sign of Castor and Pollux? Castor is the twenty-third brightest star, and it is forty- six light years from here. This brings us right back to the marriage of the virgin. The egg cell of the mother has twenty-three chromosomes; and when the sperm, with twenty-three, fertilizes it, there will be forty-six in the complete cell. The egg and sperm make a new life, and we have new life in the resurrection.

In addition, Pollux is the seventeenth brightest star and is thirty-six light years from here. If Jesus fulfilled the sign of Jonah in three full days, then He was raised on the seventeenth day of Abib. We saw how the number 18 speaks of life. Thirty-six is two times eighteen and therefore means "double life"—life in conception (new life) and life from death (resurrection).

Thus, we find the signs carefully arranged around the passion of Christ to show His death and resurrection. They show a marriage and conception. The death and resurrection of Jesus forms the central idea that the signs focus around. We will now tie together some details regarding His death and resurrection before we conclude with the Exodus.

Pollux is the fourth brightest star in the zodiac; Castor is the seventh. Jesus was in the earth three days, from the fourth day of the week until the seventh.

Jesus, the Passover lamb, was crucified on the fourteenth and raised on the seventeenth day of the month. Pollux is the seventeenth brightest star in the sky. Pollux is a sign of the Sabbath, in creation, in the law, and in the resurrection.

Next, Jesus was in the grave Abib from 14 to 17. What is 14 times 17? It's 238. Remember the 92 protons in uranium (chapter 3). Uranium has 146 neutrons that brings the atomic weight to 238. Here is another picture of marriage. Jesus was forsaken by God, so we could have hope of relationship with God and unbroken relationships.

Hence, the signs have taken us from a virgin to a bride to conception to birth. To conclude, let us note one more item.

How many kinds of blood cells are there? Seven. What day of the week did Christ die? The fourth. What day was the resurrection? The seventh. Here we find 7, 7, 4. It seems that in every picture of His face, we find these numbers, which means life. Why is blood in this picture?

**For the life of the flesh is in the blood.** (Leviticus 17:11)

**In the light of the king's countenance is life.** (Psalm 16:15) Life is in His face.

# PART 2

This section is devoted to one sign because in it, we find a picture of marriage.

> **If thou turn away thy foot from the Sabbath from doing thy pleasure on my holy day, and call the sabbath a delight, the holy of the Lord honourable, and shalt honour him, not doing thine own ways, nor finding thine own pleasure, no speaking thine own words: Then shalt thou delight thyself in the Lord, and I will cause thee to ride upon the high places of the earth.** (Isaiah 58:13; emphasis added)

The next verse is directed specifically to the *stranger*—the Gentile.

> **Also the sons of the stranger, that join themselves to the Lord, to serve Him, and to love the name of the Lord, to be His servants, every one that keepeth the sabbath from polluting it, and taketh hold of my covenant, even them will I bring to mv holy mountain, and make them joyful in my house of prayer.** (Isaiah 58:14; emphasis added)

Notice the Sabbath (a sign) will take one to the high places and to His holy mountain. God created a relationship that illustrates this. The Sabbath takes us to the high place of the earth. Pollux is the star that is a picture of the Sabbath. Pollux passes over Mt. Everest—the highest mountain.

There are three mountains of primary importance to our study of His face. The first high place is Mt. Sinai. There we found Moses receiving the law. He knew God (1 John 2:3), and his face shone. Moses had fasted eighty days, the period of abstinence for a female birth (Leviticus 12). It is interesting to note that the Sabbath brings us to the Sabbath. That is, it brings us to the high places, one of which is Mt. Sinai. At Sinai, we find the commandments, one of which is the Sabbath.

Therefore, the Sabbath multiplies itself. It is a key to what Jesus said, **"Give and it shall be given unto you"** (Luke 6:38). It is like the **"seed was in itself"** (Genesis 1:12).

The next high place is the Mount of Transfiguration. There we find that Jesus **"face did shine as the sun"** (Matthew 17:2). Jesus is the king of kings. What is in the face of a king? *Life.*

What is life? To **"know God and His Son"** (John 17:3). Moses was there with Him, the other whose face shone.

What makes a man's face to shine? Wisdom.

> **For the Jews require a sign, and the Greeks seek after wisdom.** (1 Corinthians 1:22)

The Jews required a sign—the Sabbath. The Sabbath take us to the high places, where we find His shining face. Wisdom makes a man's face to shine. The Greeks seek wisdom. Thus, Jesus fulfilled the conditions for *wisdom* and signs—for Jews and Greeks. Thus, we see that Moses knew God at the first mountain. Now we find Jesus as the groom on the second mountain. Next, the third mountain and the bride.

> **Come hither, I will show thee the bride, the Lamb's wife. And he carried me away in the Spirit to a great and high mountain, and shewed me that great city, the holy Jerusalem, descending out of heaven from God.** (Revelation 21:9-10)

Here we find the bride of the Lamb. Thus, the sign of the Sabbath has brought us to the law to "know Him" as **"Adam knew Eve...and she conceived"** (Genesis 4:1). It brought us to His face like the sun on the second mountain. Life is to **"know God and Jesus Christ"** (John 17:3), and life is in His face. Now it brings us to the bride.

There is another idea that connects the Mount of Transfiguration and the mountain mentioned in Revelation 21:9-10. What makes a man's face to shine (Mount of Transfiguration)? Wisdom. Jesus is wisdom and therefore has a crown.

**The crown of the wise is their riches.** (Proverbs 14:24)

**The rich man's wealth is his strong city.** (Proverbs 10:15)

**And the city lieth foursquare, and the length is as large as the breath; and he measured the city with the reed, twelve thousand furlongs. The length and the breadth and the height of it are equal.** (Revelation 21:16)

A furlong is 1/8 mile; the city is 1,500 miles x 1,500 miles x 1,500 miles. Obviously, a strong city of a rich man.

\* \* \* \* \*

Did you notice what the most holy place of the temple has in common with the new Jerusalem? They are both cubes with six sides.

# PART 3

Before we conclude this chapter, we would like to note some observations in passing. In this section, we want to illustrate another idea about His face and about the journey up to the mountain.

First, regarding the journey, notice what happens when people climb to great heights on mountains? They experience symptoms like drunkenness and hallucinations.

In Acts 2, when the believers were filled with the Spirit, some observers said, **"These men are full of new wine"** (Acts 2:13). They thought they were drunk. With the filling of the Holy Spirit came many visions. Thus, there is a parallel between mountain climbing and being filled with the Spirit.

Another commonality between being filled with the Spirit and climbing mountains is music. The Bible says,

> **And be not drunk with wine wherein is excess, but be filled with the Spirit; Speaking to yourselves in psalms and hymns and spiritual songs, singing and making melody in your heart to the Lord.** (Ephesians 5:18-19)

Accordingly, the graph of the equations for music resembles mountains.

Now we are ready for a look on top. Who was there? Jesus, Peter, James, John, Moses, Elijah, and God (Matthew 17:1, 3, 5). That was seven. Elijah did seven miracles during his life. Jesus's face shone as the sun. The sun was made on the fourth day of creation. Again we find the numbers 7, 7, 4 appearing around His face.

* * * * *

The sign of the Sabbath did three things:

1.  It brought us to the mystery of it replicating itself (like the blood and the Passover).
2.  It brought us to the mystery of human procreation.
3.  It brought us to the groom and the bride with the glory.

Lastly, now that we have covered this much information, look back at some of the relationships of different parts of our study. The Sabbath took us up to three mountains. The tithe took us to three vines. Notice that the combining of the tithe and the commandments leads to the rain (with the sun) and to the shining face. Thus, there seems to be a secondary point of clustering, which resonates with the life of His face.

# CHAPTER 9

## IN THE NUMBERS

There are two numbers in mathematics of primary importance—*e* and $\pi$.

$e = 2.71828182845904523...$
$\pi = 3.14159265358979323...$

Notice that both numbers end with 23 and the two in the seventeenth digit of each. Recall that we showed the resurrection of Jesus on the seventeenth day of the month as a picture of conception. Let's look closer. The *e* is most prominent in the exponential function $y = e^x$. What happens if we let *x* equal $\pi$? The value of *y* becomes 23. Let's take the number *e* and put in in the formula for a circle. Suppose we have a circle of radius *e*. This circle has a circumference of 17 and an area of 23.

Let's look at the face of Jesus in mathematics by focusing on a few examples with application from astronomy and business.

## Circles

We know that a circle is the set of all points in a plane equal distance from a given point, the center. A rainbow is circular and surrounds the throne (Revelation 3). A rainbow is like the glory of God (Ezekiel 1:28), and the "light of the knowledge of the glory of God" is in the face of Jesus (2 Corinthians 4:6). Hence, His face is the center of the circle—the rainbow.

His face is like the ark, with the glory around the ark.

## Ellipses

An ellipse is the set of all points in a plane such that the sum of the distances from two points is a constant.

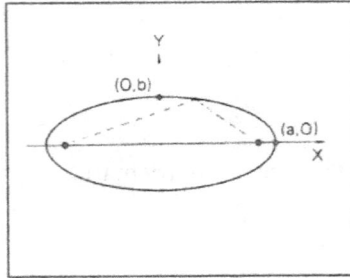

Next, His face is like the sun. The orbits of the earth and other planets around the sun are ellipses. For many years, I wondered why an ellipse has two foci but we have only one foci occupied by the sun and one vacant. The face of Jesus is like the sun. So what or who is like Jesus and yet never been seen? *The Father.*

**He that hath seen me hath seen the Father.** (John 14:9)

The mystery of the Father is illustrated with the vacant foci.

## Parabola

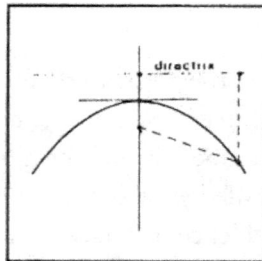

There are comets that come in with such speed that after they pass the sun, they turn and shoot out of the solar system, never to return. Their path can be one of two curves—a parabola or hyperbola.

They have a focal point which is occupied by the sun. So we found the face of Jesus in the sun and therefore in the focus of the parabola. The parabola is the graph of a quadratic equation like $y = x^2$.

Let us apply a parabola to an economic case. This type of application has unlimited possibilities—cars, clothes, food, fuel, lumber, steel, etc. It has a focus, but it cannot be the sun. I believe this represents the invisible presence of Jesus—His *face*.

Suppose a grocery sold eggs for $1 per dozen, five hundred dozen per week. Let us stipulate that for each price increase of 100, the grocery will lose forty sales. What should his price have to be to reap the best earning? This type of problem changes according to a parabola. The point of maximum earnings is at the end or top of the parabola. I believe that all economic and physical laws are derived from spiritual laws. They are material examples of spiritual principles. So gravity is a picture of a spiritual principal. Supply and demand are parables.

**For the invisible things of Him from the creation of the world are clearly seen, being understood by the things that are made, even His eternal power and Godhead; so that they are without excuse.** (Romans 1:20)

I believe that the focal point of the parabola is the face of Jesus.

Return to the example of the eggs. The eggs could just as well be cars, fuel, clothes, etc. Remember that His face is like three things—marriage, the sun, and the ark. His Word is like the seed of man. Thus, we find that we have returned to a financial benefit of children. The more children we have, the more eggs, toys, food, cars, houses, etc., we will need and hence, more work, more laborers, more jobs.

Take the parabola. Make the focal point His face or marriage. The focal point really is His face; whether it is symbolized by the sun or marriage. The economic laws are determined by Christ. He determines what part we play. He made it such that our work produces something and our children produce something.

His face is like the ark. In 2 Samuel 6, David attempted to bring the ark back to Jerusalem. As was about to fall, Uzziah put forth his hand to catch it. God struck him. David was "displeased" and "afraid" (2 Samuel 6:8-9). David left the ark in the house of Obededom instead of Jerusalem. Then **"the Lord blessed Obededom and all his household"** (2 Samuel 6:11). So there was a blessing with the ark.

When the focal point represents the face of Jesus, children, or the ark, the relation of sales to price will be on the parabola.

What we do with children, souls, and the presence and person of Christ will affect the economy. These are primary causes. What do we do in business, like $1/dozen for eggs, is a secondary cause. Thus, the economic relationships are spiritually determined.

We will include a brief study on mathematics only to suggest again the profound ramifications of His face. So we will return to the circle. Recall at the sun is like His face and the sun is round. The rainbow is like the glory of God, which is in His face, and the rainbow is circular.

A. Some general properties

As you know, a circle has 360 degrees. Angles can be measured in radians as well as degrees, 2n radians equals 360 degrees. The circumference of a circle is 2-nr. The area is $nr^2$ and $nr^2 = 1/2 (2n) r^2$.

Consider a falling body. Its acceleration will be $g$. In time ($t$), it will reach a velocity of gt, and it will have fallen a distance of $1/2 gt^2$.

Consider a moving body of mass ($m$), not necessarily falling. It's momentum is mv, where $v$ is velocity. It's kinetic energy is equal to $1/2 mv^2$.

Do you see the analogy of these three?

- 2n 2nr $1/2(2n) r^2$—circle
- g gt $1/2 gt^2$—falling object
- m mv $1/2 mv^2$—moving body

The mathematics of a falling object or a moving body can be taken from a circle. They are mathematically analogous. Furthermore, the mathematical similarity can be applied to population growth. Again, we see that marriage and procreation is the theme that explains God's construction of things, and the circle is like the sun, which is like His face.

A. Exponential function

There is a function in mathematics called the exponential. The *exponential* is an equation such as $y = ae^x$ (where $e = 2.718.$).

It just so happens that $ae^x = a + ax + {}^\wedge Aax^2$.

The elements of this sum are found in part A when we paralleled the items of a circle to physical equations.

Why is it significant that these monomials parallel the terms of an exponential? Because population grows exponentially. Wealth also grows exponentially. Why does this symmetry exist? What we do with money affects children, birth rate, and other parts of population? What we do with birth rate, children, and population will affect the economy?

The Word of God is like the seed of man. It is also like silver.

**The words of the Lord are pure words: as silver tried in a furnace of earth, purified seven times.** (Psalm 12:6)

It is an amazing fact of mathematics that once a problem is put into mathematical form and solved it, it may be identical to another problem that seems totally unrelated. In fact, they are related and therefore do impact each other. The connection is often not seen because the relation is a spiritual one.

B. $x^2 + y^2 = r^2$ and Einstein's relativity

I suppose $x^2 + y^2 = r^2$ is the most common equation of a circle. This equation can be changed in form to:

$$x = r\sqrt{1 - \Box^2/\Box^2}$$

This is analogous to the equation of relativity for length:

$$L = Lo\sqrt{1 - \Box^2/\Box^2}$$

By division, we can convert our equation tor the circle to:

$$r = \frac{x}{\sqrt{1 - \Box^2/\Box^2}}$$

This form is also in relativity. It is used for mass and time:

Notice what happens to length, mass, and time as the velocity ($v$) approaches $c$, the speed of light. Length goes to $o$ and time stops. What does that suggest? It suggests omnipresence.

The Bible says that God is light and omnipresent.

**God is light.** (1 John 1:5)

**I am the light of the world.** (John. 9:5)

**Whither shall I go from thy spirit? Or whither shall I flee from thy presence?**

**If I ascend up into heaven, thou art there: if I make my bed in hell, behold, thou art there.** (Psalm 139:7-8)

Observe what happens to mass—it becomes infinite. In Einstein's most famous equation, $E = me^2$, infinite mass means infinite energy. This suggests omnipotence, another divine property. $E = me^2$ is just like $A = nr^2$ for a circle.

**Alleluia: for the Lord God omnipotent reigneth.** (Revelation 19:6)

Thus, at the speed of light, we have omnipotence and omnipresence—two properties of God. In the equations for mass and time, if the velocity ($v$) equaled to the speed of light ($c$), there would be a division by zero, which is impossible. This illustrates the reason for this rule of division. If one divides by zero, he is dealing with things that are often divine. That is, they are things of heaven and not earth. Mathematics is for things in this universe, not for things spiritual. Thus, the limit of mathematics.

# CHAPTER 10

# LIFE

# PART 1

In this chapter, we will attempt to show the importance of life as a biblical theme. We will briefly show what produces life and what other items are connected through chains of ideas. While we look at this, observe the number of important words that are interrelated. Observe how they are all move to produce life. This section is not trying to argue how to obtain life but on how our spiritual life is strengthened or uplifted.

1. First, notice that seeing and believing are related to life. **And this is the will of him that sent me, that everyone which seeth the Son, and believeth on him, may have everlasting life.** (John 6:40; emphasis added)

2. Next, we see a reference to communion. **Verily, verily, I say unto you, Except ye eat the flesh of the Son of man, and drink his blood, ye have no life in you. Whoso eateth my flesh, and drinketh my blood, hath eternal life.** (John 6:53-54; emphasis added)

3. Next, we find humility and the fear of God leads to life. **By humility and the fear of the Lord are riches, and honour, and life.** (Proverbs 22:4; emphasis added)

The path to *life* is simple when these ideas come together:

   a. The fear of God is learned by tithing and keeping the commandments.
   b. Fasting leads to humility. **"I humbled my soul with fasting"** (Psalm 35:13).
   c. Humility and the fear of God leads to life.

It is worth noting that *fasting* is related to *health* and *healing,* **"And thine health shall spring forth speedily"** (Isaiah 58:8). This contrasts with 1 Timothy 4:8, which says, **"For bodily exercise profiteth little."** The fear of God also relates to *healing.*

> **But unto you that fear my name shall the Sun of righteousness arise with healing in his wings.** (Malachi 4:2)

There are other points that need to be included in this discussion. First, work and faith are related.

> **For as the body without the spirit is dead, so faith without works is dead also.** (James 2:26)

*Work* is necessary for the life of *faith.* Next, faith and authority are related. In Matthew 8, a centurion came to Jesus asking for the healing of a servant.

> **Jesus said, "I will come and heal him."**

> **The centurion said, "I am not worthy that thou shouldest come under my roof: but speak the word only, and my servant shall be healed.**

> **For I am a man under authority, having soldiers under me: and I say to this man, 'Go,' and he goeth; and to another, 'Come,' and he cometh; and to my servant, 'Do this,' and he doeth it."**

> **When Jesus heard it, he marveled, and said... "Verily I say unto you, I have not found so great faith, no, not in Israel."** (Matthew 8:7-10; emphasis added)

Thus, we find that *work* and *authority* are necessary to *faith*.

**For in Jesus Christ neither circumcision availeth anything, nor uncircumcision; but faith which worketh by love.**

(Galatians 5:6)

Love is necessary for faith. Hence, *love, work, authority,* and *faith* are all tied together.

In prior chapters, we tied love to the commandments with Deuteronomy 10:12-13. The commandments tell us how to fear God. The fear of God and humility produces life.

Love is tied to other ideas.

**Then came Peter to him, and said, Lord, how oft shall my brother sin against me, and I forgive him? till seven times? Jesus saith unto him, I say not unto thee, Until seven times: but, Until seventy times seven.** (Matthew 18:21-22; emphasis added)

*Forgiveness* is an important part of *love*.

**Love covereth all sins.** (Proverbs 10:12)

Love is important to faith.

**Faith which worketh by love.** (Galatians 5:6; emphasis added)

**Who through faith...stopped the mouths of lions.** (Hebrews 11:33; emphasis added)

This scripture could open avenues to several lions, but we will focus on one—the beast of Revelation 13:

**And I...saw a beast rise up out of the sea...and his mouth as the mouth of a lion...**

**Here is wisdom. Let him that hath understanding count the number of the beast: for it is the number of a man; and his number is Six hundred threescore and six.** (Revelation 13:1-2, 18; emphasis added)

Thus, we have found a chain that takes us from 490 through *forgiveness, love, faith* to 666.

Before we leave the commandments and the fear of God, there is another important item.

Jesus said, **"And ye shall know the truth, and the truth shall make you free"** (John 8:32; emphasis added). Freedom is something valued greatly by people but grossly misunderstood. What did Jesus say will make us free? The truth. What is truth?

**And thy law is the truth.** (Psalm 119:142)

**Thou art near, O Lord; and all thy commandments are truth.** (Psalm 119:151)

The law is truth, and the truth sets us free. Hence, the law and commandments are a vital and needed study. It is worth noting that since we have disrespected God's law, government control is imposing more law on the people. If we would accept God's law, we would have less government control. The commandments lead to the fear of God which, with humility, produces life.

1.  Finally, **"He that follows after righteousness and mercy findeth life, righteousness, and honour"** (Proverbs 21:21; emphasis added).

Righteousness and mercy produce *life*.

There is much richness found in study of these matters. They are primal, not incidental to our lives. Everything in this chapter connects to something that leads to life, and life is in His face.

# PART 2

We will attempt to explain what appears to be a terrain in Scripture. We believe that these verses could be the ultimate that God has for us to learn. This is not the theological or doctrinal part. It is the personal. The important questions are not on whether you do know the matters of fact and information. The important matter is do you *know* him.

There were more than 500 people who saw Jesus after His resurrection (1 Corinthians 15:6). There were 120 in the upper room on the day of Pentecost (Acts 2). At the next level, there were 70 disciples. Then we find the 12 apostles, of which Peter, James, and John were the inner circle. It was only the inner circle that was with Him on the mountain when His face shone.

This Scripture calls us "living epistles." Therefore, there is in Scripture a similar structure. It probably consists of many of the verses we have noted. Observe that many of these verses will be very familiar, but we are crystallizing them into a new pattern.

> **And this is life eternal, that they might know thee the only true God and Jesus Christ, whom thou has sent.** (John 17:3; emphasis added)

This verse is so important because it defines life eternal. Imagine that—a definition of life. It is to know God and His Son. Adam knew Eve, and she had a son. There was new physical life. When we know God and His Son, there is new spiritual life. Thus, it seems that this verse is the pinpoint, the sharpest focus, the highest pinnacle of the Bible. Everything else builds up to this verse as it's resolution.

Next, it seems that there are three verses that correspond to the inner circle of Peter, James, and John:

> **In the light of the king's countenance is life.** (Proverbs 16:15)

**And his countenance was as the sun shineth in his strength.** (Revelation 1:16)

**For God, who commanded the light to shine out of darkness hath shineth in our hearts to give the light of the knowledge of the glory of God in the face of Jesus Christ.** (2 Corinthians 4:6)

These three verses are the immediate companions to John 17:3.

Here, the theory becomes fuzzy; it begins to be more of an opinion as we proceed, but let me suggest some ideas.

There are 9 verses that correspond to the remaining 9 apostles. It seems that there is an addition to this group to make 70, which corresponds to the 70 disciples. This pattern can be continued to include the 120 (Acts 2), the 500 (1 Corinthians 15:6), etc. Thus, there seems to be an unseen terrain in the Bible—a structuring of truth.

*Life* then has one verse that defines it, John 17:3, accompanied by three others: Proverbs 16:15, 2 Corinthians 4:6, and Revelation 1:16.

Marriage, the ark, and the sun symbolize or parallel the *face*.

Jesus had three disciples in the inner circle—Peter, James, and John.

**In the light of the king's [Jesus] countenance [face] is life.** (Proverbs 16:15; emphasis added)

\* \* \* \* \*

As we said in the beginning of this chapter, the most important idea in the Bible is not what you know but if you know Him. The Scripture says, **"All have sinned, and come short of the glory of God"** (Romans 3:23). Blood was provided by the Lamb. If you will repent of your sins and turn your life over to Him, then pray this prayer:

> *God,*
> *I confess that I am a sinner. I repent of my sins. Jesus, come*

*into my heart to be my Lord and forgive me and give me new life through Your blood. Amen.*

If you prayed this prayer, I hope to hear from you. God bless you.

# EPILOGUE

The body of Proverbs is written in such a way that it will fit together in a great web of information. Historically, it predates the subject of this book, but in terms of what God wants known, the mystery of his face is more pressing and does not require the same level of secrecy. I have presented Proverbs in a way that lays a foundation for the reader to understand the secret of the Lord. So what the reader will understand about it will depend on who they yield themselves to the ways of the Lord.

The purpose of this discussion is to examine the content of Proverbs. It has an amazing pattern which leads to the secret of the Lord. We will start with Proverbs 15:26: "The words of the Lord are pleasant words," which is followed by Proverbs 16:24a: "Pleasant words are as a honeycomb," which leads to 1 Samuel 14:27: "Honey lightens the eyes," which leads to Proverbs 15:30a: "The light of the eyes rejoiceth the heart," Proverbs 15:28a: "The heart of the righteous studieth to answer," and Proverbs 16:1b: "The answer of the tongue is from the Lord."

Here's the pattern branches: Proverbs 17:3b: "The Lord trieth the hearts," Proverbs 21:2: "The Lord pondereth the hearts," and Proverbs 16:9: "A man's heart divideth his way," which is followed by Proverbs 30:19d: "The way of a man with maid." Next is Proverbs 18:22: "Who so finds a wife finds a good thing and obtains favor of the Lord," Proverbs 16:15b: "His favor is as a cloud of the latter rain," and Proverbs 5:15a: "Drink waters out of thy own cisterns."

Now we return to Proverbs 16:28a: "The heart of the righteous studieth to answer," Proverbs 15:1a: "A soft answer turns away wrath," Proverbs 16:14: "The wrath of a king is as messengers of death," and Proverbs 16:15a: "In the light of the king's countenance is life." These last two are not sequential but parallel.

They are followed by Proverbs 18:21a: "Death and life are in the power of the tongue," which is followed by Proverbs 15:4a: "A wholesome tongue is a tree of life" (though this is not part of this study, it is the logical New

Testament continuance, "Life eternal is to know God and his son, Jesus Christ").

Now let us go back to Proverbs 16:9a: "A man's heart diviseth his ways," which is followed by Proverbs 15:9: "The way of the wicked is an abomination unto the Lord," which again is followed by Proverbs 17:3b: "The Lord trieth the hearts" and Proverbs 21:2b: "The Lord pondereth the hearts."

Now let's go to Proverbs 31:10. This begins a beautiful passage of a godly woman: "Who can find a virtuous woman?" which is followed by Proverbs 12:4a: "A virtuous woman is a crown to her husband," which is followed by a good man in Proverbs 12:2a: "A good man obtaineth favor of the Lord," which leads to Proverbs 16:15b: "His favor is as a cloud of latter rain."

Now let us go back to the early part of Proverbs. In Proverbs 6, it has multiple verses of a wicked man. Proverbs 6:13a says: "He winketh with his eye," which leads to Proverbs 10:10: "He that winks with his eye causeth sorrow," which leads to Proverbs 15:13b: "By sorrow of the hearth the spirit is broken," which is followed by Proverbs 17:22b: "A broken spirit drieth the bones."

Next is Job 21:24: "His bones are moistened with marrow" (blood is made in the marrow, and before a birth, there is a bloody show and the water breaks). Now let's go back to Proverbs 6, in Proverbs 6:14a: "Frowardness is in his heart," which is followed by Proverbs 16:9: "A man's heart diviseth his ways," Proverbs 1:19: "So are the ways of everyone that is greedy of gain," Proverbs 15:27: "He that is greedy of gain troubles his house," Proverbs 11:29: "He that troubles his own house shall inherit the wind," and Proverbs 25:23: "The north wind drives away rain."

Let's look again at Proverbs 6:14a: "Frowardness is in his heart," which is followed by Proverbs 12:23: "The heart of fools proclaimeth foolishness," which is followed by Proverbs 14:24: "The foolish of fools is folly," which leads to Proverbs 14:8: "The folly of fools is deceit." This is also associated with the next two, Proverbs 14:18: "The simple inherit folly" and Proverbs 14:15: "The simple believeth every word," and this leads back to Proverbs 15:26b: "The words of the pure are pleasant words."

Now we will begin to examine a set of verses that help unify a verse that we have given regarding the good and the evil. We will start with

Proverbs 20:27: "The spirit of man is the candle of the Lord, searching all the inward parts of the belly," which is followed by Proverbs 18:20a: "A man's belly shall be satisfied with the fruit of his mouth."

Now we have another division into multiple streams. Proverbs 10:11 says: "The mouth of a righteous is a well of life," Proverbs 10:14b: "The mouth of the foolish is near destruction," Proverbs 15:11: "Hell and destruction are before the Lord," Proverbs 16:9: "A man's heart diviseth his ways," and Proverbs 15:9: "The way of the wicked is an abomination unto the Lord." Next is Proverbs 17:3: "The Lord tryeth the hearts," Proverbs 21:2: "The Lord pondereth the hearts," and Proverbs 21:1: "The king's heart is in the hands of the Lord."

On the set that includes, it is now time to continue examining the divisions of Proverbs 18:20: "A man's belly shall be satisfied with the fruit of his mouth." Let's complete this thought before we go onto the next two occurrences of mouth, and this stream splits into two other streams. Proverbs 10:15b says: "The destruction of the poor is their poverty," which is followed by Proverbs 13:18a: "Poverty and shame shall be unto him that refuses instruction," Proverbs 16:14: "The wrath of the king is as messengers of death; but a wise man will pacify it," and Proverbs 16:15: "In the light of the kings countenance is life; and his favor is as the cloud of the latter rain."

The previous two verses proceed this one, Proverbs 18:21: "Death and life are in the power of the tongue" and Proverbs 15:4: "A wholesome tongue is a tree of life."

Notice that Proverbs 18:21 begins with death and life and Proverbs 15:4 ends with life. So the concept of life begins at Proverbs 18:21 and ends at Proverbs 15:4. This is the first piece of the secret, Proverbs 15:28: "The heart of the righteous studies to answer," Proverbs 16:1: "The answer of the tongue is from the Lord," Proverbs 17:3: "The Lord trieth the hearts," Proverbs 21:2: "The Lord ponderth the hearts," and Proverbs 21:1: "The kings heart is in the hand of the Lord."

Notice that Proverbs 21:1 has the key words *heart* and *Lord* in position reversed from that of Proverbs 17:3 and 21:2, so these three make a triple that is part of a triangle with the other two legs as Proverbs 15:28 and 16:1. Notice that the information flows back and forth.

Let us return to Proverbs 31. Proverbs 31:10 says: "Who can find a virtuous woman," and next we add Proverbs 19:14: "A prudent wife is from the Lord." This occurrence of Lord connects to the beginning of Proverbs 17:3 and 21:2. Proverbs 16:9 says: "A man's heart devisith his way," Proverbs 15:9: "The way of the wicked is as an abomination of the Lord," Proverbs 17:3: "The Lord trieth the hearts," Proverbs 21:2: "The Lord ponderth the hearts," and Proverbs 21:1: "The kings heart is in the hand of the Lord."

As above, Proverbs 21:1 runs in the opposite direction from Proverbs 17:1 and 21:2 so that again, the information flows back and forth in addition to being connected in a triangular pattern with Proverbs 16:9 and 15:9. Now this paragraph appears to be identical to the one before it, but notice that one regards to godly and this one does not so. Let us imagine that this one is lying on top of the other one and then flip it over, so it is backward to us. The two triangles have their triple side face-to-face, and they are joined at the word *Lord* at the bottom and close at the top.

Having observed the organization of Proverbs, it is now possible to begin the final assimilation and study of scripture. Just as the Proverbs are linked together to make a chain, even a network of chains, thus, these chains connect to other verses throughout the Bible that makes a giant web that ties the whole Bible together. Recall Proverbs 16:15, where it says, "In the light of the king's countenance is life" and John 17:3 "Life eternal is to know God and His Son." Seeing we have finished an introduction to the face of Jesus, we are now prepared to begin a study of the Word of God.

# CONCLUSION

In the beginning, we saw that His face is like marriage and procreation. His Word is like the seed of man. Thus, the secret of His face is like marriage.

His face is like the sun. His Word is like light. Thus, the secret of His face, if understood better, can be explained as the secret of the universe.

His face is like the ark. The Word is like manna. Here can be found the mystery of the temple.

It appears that all of the secrets are one—marriage, the temple, the universe, mathematics, and money. They can be solved by His face and its analogies. If a given problem is connected to His face, then the answer will appear. That is where everything unites and reveals itself.

Before we close, we need to take a moment to address some issues.

First, His Word is like the seed of man—that is biological, that is life. It's like wheat that is agricultural—food. It's like light—that is physical, astronomical, and energy. It's like silver—that is economic. It's like a hammer—that is practical. His Word is everything. His face is everything you need.

Perhaps, the reader feels that if this is so, how do I draw on these resources? Remember the subjects we saw that led to life—tithing, the commandments, fasting,[7] Bible study, and prayer. This is a partial list, but it has some of the most important things.

Hence, it seems that all the information and knowledge is like a great Rosetta Stone. It is just different languages for saying the same thing—marriage and children—because that is what the face of Jesus is like. His face is the great fact of life.

The end.

---

[7]  Fasting is so unique. It warrants a special word here. What His face is to reality and truth, fasting is to problem-solving. In general, fasting transforms prayer from something that seems common to the miraculous. It can be for yourself or someone else. It can be deliverance from drugs, alcohol, divorce, insanity, cancer, disease, etc.

# BIBLIOGRAPHY

"Article on Nepal," in *World Book Encyclopedia.* Chicago: Scott Fetzer Co., 1993.

Abell, George O. *Exploration of the Universe.* Fourth ed. CBS College Publishing, 1982.

Haggadah

Hole, John W. Jr. *Human Anatomy and Physiology.* Second ed. William C. Brown Co., 1981.

Levi, Zola. *The Seven Feast of Israel.* 1979

Moore, Patrick. *Guinness Book of Astronomy—Facts and Feats.* Guinness Superlatives, 1983.

Norton, Arthur P., and J. Gall Inglis. *Norton's Star Atlas and Telescopic Handbook.* Cambridge, Massachusetts: Sky Publishing Corporation, reprint 1966.

US Naval Observatory. *Astronomical Almanac.* 1981.

# ABOUT THE AUTHOR

R. Nelson Prikryl grew up in Farmersville, Texas, and went on to graduate from Austin College and Christ for the Nations. R. Nelson pastored, but as he sought the Lord, he found an increasing gap between the revelation of Scripture and the traditions of the church. As he sought to be more faithful to the Word of God in dropping the tradition, he found the beautiful truth of the wisdom and knowledge of God in the face of Jesus.

CPSIA information can be obtained
at www.ICGtesting.com
Printed in the USA
BVHW030616230922
647758BV00017B/1342